Lost and Finding

Priyadharshini Rajagopal

Presentation by *BookLeaf Publishing*

Web: www.bookleafpub.com

E-mail: info@bookleafpub.com

ISBN: 9789363312647

First edition 2024

I dedicate this book to all the Third Culture Kids

ACKNOWLEDGEMENT

To my sister, Prashanthini, who claims she's the closest thing to my DNA. Your understanding of my world is unparalleled.

To my mom, Uma, who nudged me towards all the passions I now cherish, especially writing.

To my dad, Rajagopal, who may scoff at fiction but reads my work nonetheless, your support means everything.

To my brother-in-law, Mugesh, for patiently listening to my orations over and over till the rhyming is just right.

To my Grandpa, whose animated tales of Indian mythology ignited my imagination and sparked my love for our ancient literature.

To my dearest friends scattered across the globe—Alefia, Shivani, Reshma, Devyani. In a world of billions, finding you was a stroke of luck beyond measure.

To my cousins, Varshini, Harini, and Seerthi, whose laughter and endless conversations made every summer in India an unforgettable joy ride.

To my cousins, Subashini and Shalini, fellow Third Culture Kids with whom I shared the unique experience of living in two postings together—what an extraordinary coincidence!

PREFACE

Most of the experiences that you find in the poems actually happened to me. It isn't easy to find someone who has traveled and lived so widely across continents in their childhood years. And if you do, it is far and few.

I know there are several TCKs and expat children who are also looking for someone to connect with and talk about their shared unique and rare experiences. This book is an attempt to rediscover those unique and often contradictory feelings. In this book, I also explore the intricacies of the various inequalities that I have observed across the world and how universal these feelings of disparity are.

This book is the result of 21 days of staying up late, bugging my family to listen to what I wrote, and countless cups of coffee!

The New Kid

All eyes fall on me,
the noisy classroom's cacophony
goes silent suddenly,
when I enter the room solely
not because I'm popular,
but because,
I'm that new kid here,
the one that joins mid-year.

Like a voyager from a distant shore,
where tales of the sea are more,
fidgeting and unsure,
wondering who'll be kind enough
to let me sit next to them
and intrude upon their
already perfect circle of friends,
almost like a collection of their gems.

Can anyone hide their desperation,
to be accepted in this situation?
my eyes plead and seek,
for someone to invite me
to sit next to them
if only for a week.

And as always,
I find that one gentle soul,
another outsider like me
who becomes my friend.

I have always befriended outsiders
those who feel they don't belong
are the people with whom I feel the most at
home
no longer so alone,
with much trouble, I have found
some semblance of comfort zone.

Days spent correcting my name,
weeks catching up, in the school game,
months later,
I'm a bit less tame,
a little less of a mess.

I try to break character
and see if I can ever be

the popular and cool one,
but as always,
in every country,
in every grade,
I am called the quiet and shy one.

It is easy to find your core
personality in such instances
for in every environment,
parts of you don't change
independent of external circumstances.

Maybe one day I'll find my true face,
where I'm not the outsider in the race,
where I'm not shy, or misplaced,
the search continues,
for that beautiful surreal place.

Race

R a c e
In big letters, it filled the whiteboard
for the whole class and beyond to see
Welcome on board!
It was in the first grade,
of The International School of Ulaanbaatar
When this four-letter word
was introduced to me

My first-grade teacher
carefully explains,
This is not the kind
of race you run on the playground
or bets on who comes first
she begins to quench our curious thirst

R a c e,
She began
are a group of people of common ancestry
we are all different and unique,
Children of Diversity

R a c e.
She talked about Whites or Caucasian
then Blacks and Asians
Latinos and Pacific Islanders
to us little bundles of wonder
the very first time
I saw my school friends differently
an unspoken thing, I knew it was there,
when a word was given to
a fleeting thought floating in the air,
I felt my thoughts finally condense
things began to make sense
the freckles on Adam,
the voluminous Afro of Abba,
silky straight tresses of Xia
a class teeming with such distinct lineage

We are teaching you about race
and not school tests you must ace
for some hurtful things have been said
to your classmates of similar age

Like, "You can't play with ice
because you are Mongolian," or
"I don't like her because she is dark and feels
like an alien"
with this attitude, in the real world, we shan't
embark

We must now put a full stop, mates
to racism within our own school gates
each one of you is deserving of equal treatment
and we are here to provide
a safe and respectful environment

No matter where someone is from
black, white or brown,
you must respect one another
because everyone is equal
and beautiful in this town

I don't want to hear again,
about kids saying mean things,
if it should happen again,
think of the hurt your words might bring.

Today I wish for my first-grade teacher
to be the president of planet Earth.
If that were to happen,
the world will be filled alike with merry and
mirth.

Homesick

I envy those who are
Blessed enough to get homesick
Like a flu that comes and goes
For I too get homesick
But without the conviction of
Where that home is.
It feels more like a chronic ailment
For which there is presently no cure

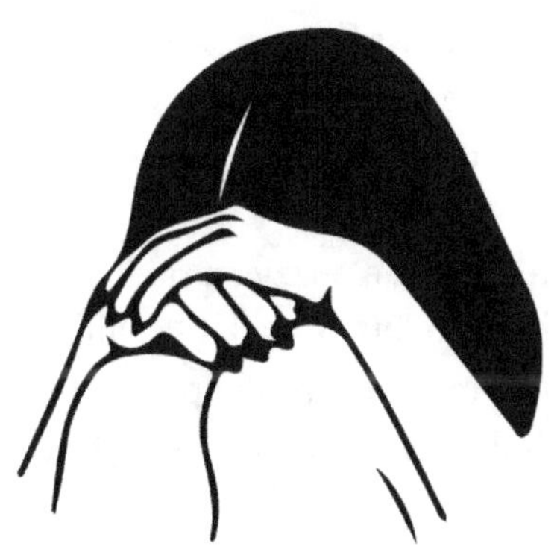

Middle School Locker

In fifth grade at Annandale Elementary,
Middle school lockers held a strong allure,
A symbol of teenage responsibility,
A place to escape life's weight and more,
Where my mind could finally be free and soar.

Middle school awaited, a new chapter to start,
Lockers whispered secrets to an eager sixth
grader's heart.

The combination, a puzzle, a riddle untold,
Turn right, then left, then right again, and clink
Each clink, a victory, a triumph to behold,
In the echoing hallways, where mysteries
unfold.
Hallways that were heavily patrolled
By middle school teachers,
Who impressed upon us with all their might
to always "keep to the right."

From textbooks to treasures, it housed my array,
Of novels and notes to brighten my day.
Colored pens and binders, a mirror for quick
check,
Motivational posters, poems on a sticky note
deck.

Through sixth, seventh and eighth grade
It held my school tale,
With my Flute, sketches,
some classic paperbacks, ambitions set sail.
From science trophies to honour roll badges,
It witnessed my many accolades,
A sanctuary during school days,
Where dreams can take rest
And conquer the halls the next day
When it re-opens for me to be my best.

So here's to my locker, a space of my own,
In the bustling corridors where memories were
sown.
A haven of unbridled growth, where ambitions
unfurled,
In the halls of Annandale, the heart of my
middle school world.

Lunch Table of the Indian Sub Continent

My dear friend from Pakistan, Maya
And from Afganistan, Zahida,
We always sit next to each other during lunch
hours
We talk animatedly about Desi sweets
From back home in the busy local streets
And how a B-plus on a test
To our father, is a hyperloop
to the Safeway cash counters
God Forbid!

When we chat
We chat for hours
About how similar we are
Almost like finding ourselves in a sea of others
As we exchange thoughts
I learn more about her world
And she about mine
Without the Line of Control
Ever coming between us
I find that the borders
Are thicker in our minds
Than on any map in existence

The Language of Third Culture

When I speak English
I am transported back to my literature class
discussing the existential
and debating on deeply dividing topics,
Sylvester Stallone's blows and kicks
from the classic film Rocky
remains still, the choicest picks
I allow myself to be captured by
The magic of Lion King
and the Heroism of Batman
an era of long frocks and English hats
Hopscotch and twister mats

When I speak Hindi,
I'm back in New Delhi,
playing the street game of pittu or lagori,
stacking seven flat stones
before you throw your ball at me
and claim chest-thumping glory
I am at my Mira Model School
writing essays on 'mere priya tyohar'
with my hand inexperienced in Hindi words
and how to use an ink pen
Throwing water balloons on Holi ka din,
bursting rockets in the Diwali sky
watching the gigantic Raavan burn
on the Dusshera day tyohar
buying the special Shakalaka Boom Boom
pencil
from the nearby shop called Kartar
that will make all your drawings come alive.
I am a player in the game of Tambola
with lucky number seven and hum paanch five
drinking cool lassi on a hot day
swaying to the tunes of Hindi Cinema
what a memory, the dance moves of Govinda!

When I speak Tamil
I am transported to my mother's arms,
where hugs are a balm
and love is bountiful and abound

The sharp whistlings, the melodic music scores
once you enter a cinema hall and leave behind
all your woes
Be enraptured by the glam sham of Rajnikanth,
The unbeatable Tamil Super Star
The taste of warm filter coffee
in a brass tumbler,
Buying a bunch of jasmine flower
beneath the temple banyan tree
where we sometimes sit and listen
to the temple bells ring
The sound of wishes being granted,
such is the peace that it can bring
My mom massaging my hair
with generous coconut oil
complaining why I don't use it enough
The innumerable times I struggled to keep my
sambar
within the borders of my banana leaf
I will forgive you, my beautiful banana plate
wherever I am in the world
when sick and health hold me for ransom,
It demands only and only
tamarind infused rasam

It's like Narnia's magic unfurled,
pick a language
and immerse into a different world.
But most of all,

The language of Third Culture
is kind and sweet, like honey,
for they see the world
for the first time—
all innocent and uncritical

It is and Is not

To travel the world is to embrace a moment's
grace,
where society's rules lose their place.
where the stark lines of right and wrong fade,
where the "correct" and "incorrect"
the "should be" and "has to be" cease to matter

Because for every "should be"
there exists an example of "is not"
and for "every incorrect"
the incorrect still exists, rightfully so

Your "must be this" and
"must be that"
are met with a defiant "is not"

Will you dare with nature's might,
to create something better, in your sight?

Belongings

I have done this,
Maybe a hundred thousand times,
But it never gets old,
Like familiar chimes.

It's that time of the year again,
Put into boxes is your entire home,
Filled with memories penned,
To be packed and shipped, to roam.

The books I never part with
The flute I used to play with
The clothes I've outgrown,
The bedsheets I've known.

I desperately try to pack as much,
As humanly possible in my house,
But as always, there are some things,
That get left behind.

The closet where I hid to scare
My sister with a fright,
The safe place under my bed
Where I kept my scribbles tight.

The window blind that lets in light,
Casting shadows on my wall,
The place where I measured my height,
My name scribbled tall.

Of all the things I leave behind,
Friends are the hardest to part,
Dozen goodbyes feel too unkind,
No one prepares your heart.

It hits me
I'll probably never return again.
On that last trip through the city,
The joys, heartbreaks, and the pain,
Races through my inexperienced heart
All consume me in their pity.

Memories take me back
To the very first day of May,
Now it's the last day,
Last hour, and last moment
Till the flight takes off
From the runway

Once again, Goodbye Forever,
To the place where memories sever.

MOVING WEST

Not Western enough to be Western
Not Indian enough to be Indian,
As I pledge allegiance to the flag
Of the United States of America
The lines of Jana Gana Mana
Run in my mind parallelly
I wear a T-shirt and jeans
Sometimes forgetting to wipe away the red
kumkum on my forehead
And when I do,
I walk around
As if I had a rash
But only between my eyebrows
In the star-spangled hallways of my school

CONCEPT

For the longest time
The concept of India
Has felt more imaginary
Than a real sense of identity
For my experience in my country had been
A couple of summer holidays at best
But with my passport Indian
And my mother tongue Tamil
I bleed blue during the Cricket World Cup
So surely, I am an Indian
Despite having never felt the legitimacy
Of representing my own country

My Happy Place

Would it be the snow-covered heights,
Ladakh's mountains, majestic sights,
Niagara's cascading falls
Or the world's biggest malls
Safaris of Serengeti,
Forests of giant pandas
Or the seven hills of Uganda

So tempting, yet my happy place,
Was never found in nature's embrace.
My dreamland, from the start,
Is a library filled with works of pure art
Where books are stacked
All the way up to the ceiling so high
A ladder is needed to reach their height

Not a haphazard one
Where romance mingles with sci-fi
And dystopian with fantasy,
But a neatly arranged one
Following the Dewey Decimal system
With a librarian
Who tells everyone to hush
And where silence rules the air

Different chairs
For different moods
As it often happens in life
The seasons keep turning
Grippy stools for focus,
Bean bags for reading
After a midday siesta,
A cocoon-like seat
For tales of loss and love
And a special carpeted spot
For readings on spiritual paths
And findings

Visitors come, seeking in turn,
References, inspiration to learn,
Humour to brighten each passing day,
Words of strength to guide in the day
and sometimes through all of life,
A companion to share your joys and sorrows
For life is happening now,

And not a sequence of tomorrows.

A friend that will give you company
In happiness and sadness.
A friend that lets you into their world
And takes you away from your worries and
hardships

This library is very dear to me,
Like a god-sent fairy,
A safe haven where no one will yell at me
For reading way too much
And writing passionately in my diary
Where silence is a virtue
And those who talk too much
Will be gently taken away
For its a well-known blasphemy
And the gatekeepers need
To protect the library's sanctity

Where imagination takes sail
Ideas, compassion and perspectives prevail
For it connects readers and writers alike,
In this sanctuary, where minds take flight.

OUTAGE

Some people lose things,
Bit by bit,
One at a time,
Like plucking petals,
Of a flower, one after another,
Continuing to preserve a sense of regularity.

But I notice,
That I lose things all at once,
Over and over,
Like a power outage,
In a big city.

Cricket Through the Night

One day, my dad took us
to the village where he grew up
Whenever the village loses power,
We gather 'neath the night's dark seam,
From our homes, out to the fields we tread,
With torchlights, and two straw chairs instead,
An old newspaper fans the warm air,
As crickets chirp with night's declare

A thunderous roar rips the sky
Lightning flashes split the dark
Through the night, crickets sing their song,
A chorus that lulls all night long.
In their chirps, a safety is found
In the deep darkness, a comforting sound.

Heartbeats of the night, steady and clear,
In their chorus, the villagers' fears are allayed
"I'm here," they say, "I'm here," they call,
Through the night, till dawn's first fall
Their symphony, a nocturnal friend,
Guides us till light, till night's end.

FLEETING

When I love
I love things so deeply
It scares me
For I know this too
Will not last
Nothing ever does
But the crime here is
How unforgivably
Short-lived my love is.

KING OF HEARTS

Love is
Contradictory

For You,
who wishes
to conquer her,
will never be able
to reign over her,
No matter what you do

You, who unclips her wings
to let her soar and fly high,
to be the queen of the skies,
will be the king
that rules her heart

And through this,
she becomes
yours forever.

Meanderings of my Love

You don't get to tell me
how to love
For only I know the depths
of my affection
Just as you would never really know
By looking at the sea,
Just how deep the ocean bed can be

And what may seem shallow
can be the gateway to my gallows
For you don't know where the trenches are,
you see
The things left behind by stormy seas

Love is consistency
sewed in everyday life
Like the morning dailies

accompanied with bread and butterknife
Opening the windows to your home
letting in sunlight and the neighbourhood you've
known

Love is mystical and magical
like children stories
and classic fairytales
Love is real,
as real as sitting cross-legged beside you
in your sickness, holding you dear

It can be liberating
like finding wings to fly with
Or suffocating
like sinking in quicksand
It can tickle you like a peacock feather
or fill you with death
like running fingernails down a chalkboard
shall you dare to come hither

It is a touch of kindness,
It's a simple "I understand you"

It's a lavish candlelight dinner
with a sumptuous buffet
offering the best, most exotic
from all over the world

It can also be
a plate of pastry split in two,
offering kindness, without knowing you
A reassurance of "I'm there for you"
A midday jog in the neighbourhood park,
A midnight run to a roadside ice cream cart
Leave everything behind,
Let the stars guide us, into the night we chart

It could be a 90's song,
familiar and at home,
It can also be meta, deep and dense
a challenge to your musical sense

Love can be a promise of a lifetime
till death do us part,
It can also be parting ways
For if I cannot bring happiness
perhaps something else out there may

Hearts of Plastic

Some souls are light,
fluffy and free
Most are drawn to them but not me,
God help me, for
I am taken by the latter

I gravitate towards
the outliers,
the rebels,
the ones who always come last
I wonder what shadows of pain haunt their past.

The ones who don't conform,
rather cannot conform
But they exist,
Like a red traffic signal,
That makes you

stop and take a pause
Are they wrong,
Or are we all wrong?

The world is not friendly to all
who is to say
what's normal and what's not?
For every human is a creation of nature
and nature can never go wrong
It is us and only us
who can make a person
feel all so wrong.

The ones who chew gum
in the face of fate,
the ones who block out
the whole universe with their
deafening headphones
and their carefree gait,
The ones who pair the
most bizarre combination of
clothes and style the
most outlandish hairstyles
The ones to show up at a party
just to say goodbye

To go to a party
was like going to war,
I prefer war,

to sitting at a table
full of strangers,
laughing, giggling, smiling
and clinking wine glasses

I used to once fantasize about being the
happening socialite,
who goes to all these dinner parties
and then I did become that person
It lasted but briefly

Behind plastic smiles and crafted lies,
of being sorted and settled
There is just despair in disguise,
cutlery clinks, phony laughs
and announcements of
"I've made it in life"
fill the plastic air

The bold-colored lipstick and pricey handbags
reminds me of a dollhouse
on the shelf of a toy store
but without the happiness

As I am sitting there
with people who think that they are woke,
I dream of going to bed already
for even my dreams and nightmares
feel more real than these blokes

After one fine dinner party,
I decided I didn't want
dozens of friends
All I want is one true friend
where even toiling is fun
and a place where laughter never ends
I would choose that
to anything else under the sun

My party is
being with that one person
At home
spreading peanut butter on bread
watching my favourite show
laughing truly and wholly
from the soul
to the dialogues of my favourite characters
In this moment,
holds an eternity of happiness

FIREFLIES

Why are you hungry
for the attention of others?
Why cross your arms
and wait for another
to tell you about the qualities you possess?
Why long for someone to come along,
to validate that you belong?
Isn't it obvious, can't you see?
Or is it still not clear to thee?

Do things exist only
under light's illumination?
For this, I was never drawn to sunflowers
so reliant on the sun's dictations
a life chained
to the motions of another body
Even the grand oceans fail to impress,
For they are hooked to the

moods of the moon
Even the moon's beauty
is just a sunlit facade,

Why wait for
the sun to discover you,
and leave it
to the discriminating light
to bounce off parts of you

How freeing it would be,
to be just a firefly,
lighting the world as it flutters by.
How spectacular if everyone glowed,
outshining the star-studded night sky
Why not bring the Big Dipper down,
to the land where you wear your crown?

See how fireflies illuminate,
the forest's deepest darkest parts
What a beautiful, mystical sight,
a self-lit existence, pure and bright.

Disintegrating

Uncertainty is scary,
believe me, I know
for I know not, to which part of the world
a whole part of my life would go
but certainty is scarier still,
when a certain amount of certainty sets in
it gives a chill.
Oh my, what panic, what a fright,
like an evil whisper in the night.

It's like someone told you the climax
of your novel's final great twist,
and now it's the last chapter,
and no more stories exist.

Nothing is sadder, nothing more bland,
than walking through life with everything
planned.
That's why stability is so unnerving,
why people shatter lives so deserving.

They break their white picket fences down,
and start again, in a different town.
This time, let's do things differently,
be braver, take chances fervently.

Go back to being broke,
hungry for the first note,
For in the unknown, we find our drive,
it's there that we truly awaken and come alive.

It's amazing that
so much of life is about
yearning for acceptance and assimilation
only to realise
you are now pining for disintegration.

Stormy Particles of Dreams

Everyone has dreams
Some are bigger than others
I don't know if dreams are liberating
Or routinely imprisoning
But those who hold dreams
Seem to suffer more
After all, what are these dreams made of really?
How does it feel, sound or smell
And who put that
In our hearts to dwell?

So what if dreams don't come true
Too many dreams are already frozen over
For winter has arrived
And now we can't go back
So now you
Just live until one day you don't.

But when dreams
Are so out of sync
with reality,
You feel like an imposter
Living someone else's life
Like accidentally walking into the wrong class
And you just stayed there

For the whole year
And no one had a clue
No one knows your hidden strife,
You're drowning every day
In a secret life.

You lie to yourself, say you're fine,
say you have no dreams, just biding time.
List "Ten things I'm grateful for,"
Cheer up, hold your chin up.

Until one day, you stumble upon your dream
And it makes you see the world again—
Like a new born,
A happiness you thought long gone,
Like the last leaf clinging on.

It's not just any day,
But the last of autumn's sway,
The last leaf holds tight,
As snow blankets the night.
Seeing other trees go bare
And as piles of snow gather on its branches
I decide to take my chances.

The leaves grow green and pure
Life is lush and abundant once more
But dreams have an inert property
Of exploding into every inch of your world

As you know it.
It comes in like a hurricane
And takes away everything on its path.

But how do you even know
What kind of dreams burn inside her?
For even eyes lie so beautifully, as seasons
unfold.

My Design is Not My Fate

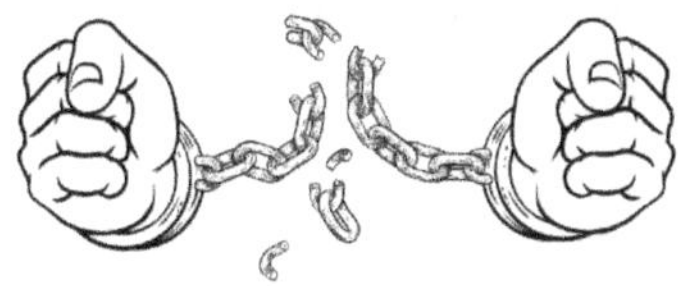

At age five
I knew girls and boys were different
Almost like we come from different planets
No wonder they say
Girls are from Venus and boys, from Mars,
They say we are all the same
But the truth is we are not.

Be it soccer, badminton or basketball
Boys just do it better
So it seems settled, once and for all
For they are faster and more powerful
Of course, there are exceptions
But maybe I wasn't one.

I questioned the Gods,
Why have you created such weakness in women
And a design so sour,
Why have you created such a disparity in
strength

Wherein men can easily overpower.

You have bestowed men
With a natural gift of command
And us with a curse of giving

Men rise to positions of power
Like bubbles in boiling milk,
And we rise like scaling rugged walls
Clambering for feeble rocks.

Fear not, you wishful heart,
I challenged the divine design,
I am unfazed by how effortlessly you climb,
If I have to reach where you are
I would rather bear a hundred thousand
More cuts and half a million more bruises
Than consider the thought,
That perhaps I am weak,
And accept a life of defeat.

Bravery is not a mere
Showcase of raw muscle or might
It's not a brutal knock-down
Or a call for a final showdown.

It is overcoming
Your doubts in a fight
And I have been plagued with many doubts

Like a dormant volcano holding down its
monster
It's strange that I have also
A self-replenishing well of self-confidence
And a never-depleting spring of belief

Be warned, my opponent!
Don't be deceived by my design,
For my design is not my fate
And if you judge poorly rather,
You may be met with a surprising match.

I enter the ring hiding my fear
Looking steady and bold,
And the puzzling fear in your eyes,
In the absence of mine,
Is pure gold.

Little do you know
I have been scared
For far too long,
To let fear ever rule over me.
For if I let fear rule me,
I would be dead by now.

BORN TO SMILE OR
BORN TO BE REAL

Was it written
In the Ten Commandments,
That girls should smile,
And adorn themselves
With shiny glossy ornaments
With bracelets
That feel like handcuffs
And chokes
That do just that

A blouse so tight
Breath dare depart your lungs
Hair extensions that
pin your thoughts down

like arrows that make a lunge

Incomplete without bangles
Unfinished without a necklace
Unkempt without certain paraphernalia
Am I wrong or
No human should feel incomplete
Without these metallic regalia

Be it India, East Africa
Even the United States of America,
Girls are often under a harsh spotlight,
Every raised eyebrow seen as a blight
Every curve or pursing of the lips
Measured, judged and put to test
White or Black, no one here is blessed
When under the spotlight,
I see you turn the color of fear
Two things can happen in this circle of light
beaming
A perfect recital born of sheer fright,
Lines delivered, but empty of meaning
Or a grand performance, applause in the hall,
A standing ovation, the curtain call

Or the light can be too bright to bear,
Expectations too heavy for a spirit so fair.
The script doesn't latch onto your tongue
You stammer several dozen times

A severe departure from your lines.
You have brought to the stage utter chaos
A terrible devotee to the play,
I see it's time to be my own boss
For I deviate from the script way too much
Even improv seems to be thrown off by me

How many powder room gossips
On the length of her hair
The size of her bosoms,
The curve of her bottoms
A little less, a little more
Too much or too less
Like finishing an artwork
For others to experience

What if she has no interest
Whatsoever,
In such
Shallowed, hollowed existence?

What if she wants to leap from
The fixed hammered frame,
Exonerate herself from these
Two-cents-worth games,
And walk free into the real world
Full of real things
And live life that's more real
And not for a show of fame

Time and again
She is asked to be "balanced"
Has anything of passion
Ever been achieved by balance?
She concludes but with a heartache
Perhaps it's to ensure
Nothing of passion even gets to see daybreak

We are asked
To keep our minds open
But sometimes,
It feels like we are asked
To keep all of ourselves empty
Like vessels

So we can contain the
Needs and desires,
The likes and dislikes
Of others.

THE END OF THE TCK JOURNEY

The words have barely
Parted with my tongue
Before the slightest utterance,
Goodbye once again
Before I fully grasp
What I have left behind,
I am bombarded with a new life
That stares me in the face

This *leaving* happens
Every two or maybe three years
Like the commas in a sentence
Arresting a train of thought
All of a sudden,
When the moving stops

And it's time to say farewell
To this Third Culture life
It feels like a full-stop
That you never anticipated
And
All the goodbyes
Said and Unsaid
Hit you all at once.

An Adult TCK (Third Culture Kid)

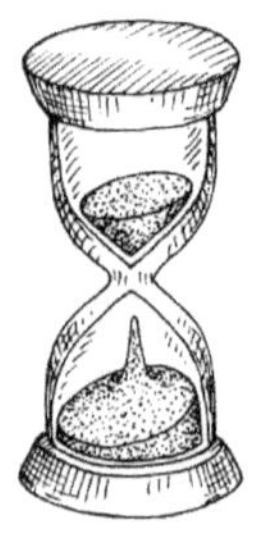

I no longer lug my luggage
from city to city
no longer hold my passport
tightly to my chest
when I move from country to country

I only drag my car
from home to office
and from office to home
braving the city's unforgiving traffic

I am asked where I am from
And I say the city
and put a full stop to that.

No one can know
my little secret

not sure why
but it feels like
I am an intruder in my own country
for I can see
the color of your face change
when I list the places
I actually hail from

And the distance between
you and me widens
with every country I say,
Your eyes set the gap between us,
as you realise we're worlds apart,
I feel like I'm losing you bit by bit,
and it breaks another piece of my heart.

I hate that look of realisation
for it spells yet another
circle that I won't be a part of
Another budding friendship
that comes to an ending.

People who look lost, like me,
are the ones I am most likely to befriend,
but they're hard to find, you see,
most seem to find their flock in the end.
and the ones that remain
after the rigorous sieving
If any, become my friends.

I have been more lucky
in some destinations than others,
It is a process that involves
an incredible probability
but this insane probability has
happened to me a few times
and for that, I will be
eternally grateful in these rhymes.

Bactrian Camel

If I should have a spirit animal
It shall surely be the Mongolian camel

The two humps
Like the two baggage I have lugged around
When travelling across lands
I too am a ship sailing through sand dunes
But without a compass
Covering seemingly endless swathes of sand
Without any track or path
Hoping somewhere, someday I may find an
oasis
It comes but rarely and
Forever shifting
But when it does, I pack as much of the oasis
Into my wayward two humps
And draw from it during my periods of drought
Till I find my next oasis.

Belonging nowhere, a Nomadic existence
But somehow withstanding everywhere
Looking strange and odd, not majestic
nor pleasing to the eye
I am not what will brighten your day
But to dispel the dark, I may

Bulging from everywhere
Soaking up whatever I find in my environment
I trot unassumingly with my God-given design
I have not the mane of a Lion,
the colors of a peacock,
Or the venom of a snake
But I am made of something
that cannot easily break.

I trust my Bactrian way, my wayward shape

Fighting the merciless winter nights of Inner
Mongolia
And the blistering sun of the Gobi Desert
The cold shoulders of loneliness
Or the heat of social judgement
I trot unassumingly with my wayward design
Don't you ever wonder
what it would take to break me?

To the majestic animals
Of jungles or mountains,
Know that I am not made
For a fragile existence
You cannot domesticate me
As easily as you did
with my dromedary single-humped friends
I belong nowhere but to the wild
And just a few of us remain in the end

Show me your harshest extremes
I shall trot in your extremes
Unassumingly with my wayward design.

My Home is You

Dearest Sister,

You were always there
from the very beginning of my memories
I even remember you strolling my pram
Taking me away from my little worries
Do you remember us collecting Pokemon cards
and "Gotta catch 'em all!" we sang
what about trying to catch butterflies in a jar
At the break of spring

I remember you were the more artistic one
and I was the assistant
I watched you color the white paper the color of
sun

and entrust me with a square inch of that
and let me think my contribution was important

I remember how we fought
and wished death on each other
And how patch-ups
were as certain as the sunrise and sunset
For a world without you
is not a world worth fighting for

When the world is scary
full of mean people and mean things
I run back to you
And suddenly the world ceases to be frightening
I remember that gaping void
when you left for college
stuck without you in our bedroom
looking at the twin bed where you used to sleep
with your *Harry Potter and the Chamber of
Secrets*

And even after the lights go out
we used to chat for hours on end
sometimes I pretend you are still there
rolling your eyes at me
as I tell you how my day went

I remember you, patiently
for hours pulling bubblegum

off my hair
My eyes pouring streams of tears
fearful that I would have to
chop my hair off and go bald from here

Time pulls us farther and farther apart
But what would I not give for
you to roll your eyes at me and wish me death
I love you to the Neptune and back
because Pluto is not a planet
see how much has changed
since we were little kids

The only home I know is you.